# DECISION MAKING

By the Spirit

## BECKY FISCHER

FOR THOSE WHO ARE LED
BY THE SPIRIT OF GOD
ARE THE CHILDREN OF GOD.

Romans 8:14

Decision Making by the Spirit
Copyright © 2014
Written by Becky Fischer
Published by Kids in Ministry International, Inc.
PO Box 549, Mandan, ND 58554

Unless otherwise stated, Scripture quotations are taken from the
New International Version by Zondervan, Grand Rapids, MI

Cover image by CanStockPhoto.com
Artist: AnatolyM

Kids in Ministry International
website: www.kidsinministry.org
For information call 701-258-6786 or
Email: kidsinministry@yahoo.com

No part of this book may be reproduced or transmitted in any form or by any means, electronic, mechanical, including photocopying, recording or by an information storage and retrieval system for the purpose of profit making without permission in writing from the author.

[I] DO EXACTLY WHAT MY FATHER
HAS COMMANDED ME.

John 14:31

# DECISION MAKING BY THE SPIRIT

Our lives are the sum total of the decisions we have made, both good and bad, from childhood till now. Poor decision making has ruined and stifled millions of lives, including true Christians. Sincere followers of Christ are not immune to making bad choices.

Most of us at one time or another made rebellious, prideful decisions when we knew better. But these are not the ones I am be referring to. This discussion covers those where we have truly wanted to follow God, and obey Him, but just didn't get it right. How does that happen when you are really trying to hear God's voice?

## REVELATION CHANGED MY LIFE

I was in my thirties before I heard any practical teaching on how to be led by the Spirit of God. Up to that point, all I knew was to be led by open and closed doors. The only problem with that is Satan can also open and close doors just as easily as God can. So then it is a matter of determining who is opening which doors. But when I began to get solid, scriptural teaching on the subject, the revelation of being able to recognize God's voice and determine what He was saying literally changed my life.

The Bible actually has a lot to say on being led by the spirit of God, and Jesus himself said, "I do nothing and say nothing but what I hear the father say and do." John 5:19 Later he said, "That the world may learn that I love the Father and [I] do exactly what my Father has commanded me. John 14:31

What would our lives look like if from this moment on we made a pledge in our hearts to do the same—to never make a decision without knowing God's direction? Many of us want to, but too often don't know how He speaks, so we don't even know how to recognize His voice.

## HE'S OUR EXAMPLE

If we can only learn to only base our decisions on what we hear from spirit of God, and only move when he tells us to move, it would be a game changer for most of us. I suspect that actually most of us at one point or another, do hear the voice of God, but we don't like what we hear. So we choose to go our own way. Of course, there is a price to pay for that.

As a result we get what can be called good old fashioned "experience." Experience is what you get when you didn't get what you wanted. There's a better way! And it's God's way. Hopefully we will be quick learners and learn from our mistakes. But how much better to make as few mistakes as possible.

There are practical tips in Scripture to teach us how the Holy Spirit speaks. Many of us have at least head knowledge of them, even if we have not learned how to practically apply them in our lives. They include things like knowing God has a still small voice or a gentle whisper (1 Kings 19:12). Scripture says he will lead us beside still waters which coincides with the scripture that says he leads us by peace (Isaiah 55:12). We know the scripture talks about a spiritual magnetic pull, which is how He draws us close to Himself by his spirit (John 6:44). One of the most common ways He spoke in Scriptural times was through dreams and visions. There are lots of books and sermons on these subjects, and many saints operate freely in these special abilities. In the Old Testament, God would often say to the prophets, "What do you see?" One familiar example is with young Jeremiah in the first couple of chapters of his book.

God asked him twice in the same chapter, "Jeremiah, what do you see?"

"This is what I see, Lord." And He would describe them.

"You have spoken well," God answered, "and I'm watching over my word to perform it." (Jeremiah 1:11)

He spoke often in symbolic pictures, then expected the prophets to interpret and discover what He was trying to say to them. Even our children can learn how to interpret dreams and visions when taught on age appropriate levels.

## THE DEEPEST PART OF US

In our Kids in Ministry International children's ministry curriculums and lessons, we teach children that He speaks to our spirits down in our innermost being, down on the deepest inside of us, like the yoke of an egg is in the deepest place.

Another example I use with them is the use of electric street lights. The red light or the "stop" light, in our hearts is God's way of telling us to stop the direction we're going in, and do something different. We can recognize it in our spirit because it feels yucky, like a knot in our stomach, or in some cases as intense as an internal tornado. It's an uneasy feeling.

On the other hand, a green light, or the "go" signal, is warm, and peaceful, that familiar calm assurance that we get, but we know we're in his will. It is His peace.

Whether the red or green signal, it's more of a feeling rather than a voice. This is where some people make their mistake. There are actually listening for a voice they can hear with the ears in their head. But His voice comes to us in the ears of our spirits most of the time. If you look at the examples I've listed above, His voice is not actually a voice. It's an impression, or a gut feeling on the inside, similar to an "intuition." That's why it can be a little tricky at times. Especially because it can be easily confused with our human emotions which may not have anything to do with the Spirit of God. Of course, whatever one senses, it always has to line up with God's Word to us.

Learning to be led by the spirit of God, and listening to his voice for direction, is one of the most important things Christians can attempt. We would all make fewer mistakes in life. We would get involved with fewer of the wrong people, accept fewer of the wrong jobs, not go to the wrong colleges, not date the wrong people, and get in less trouble in business, finances, marriages, and more, if we would determine in our hearts to listen and obey the voice of God. I've often wondered if Christians knew how to hear the voice of God more clearly, would they have married the person they did? (Are you smiling?) How much heartache could that save?

Because most of the things I've mentioned so far are taught on frequently by others, I'm not going to go into them any deeper today. Instead I want to cover things not typically presented on this topic. While many of us have had teaching on many of the things I've mentioned so far, yet, many times we still can fall prey to the same mistakes as those who know very little. We must ask why? This is what I want to talk about today. Is there anything else we can learn on this subject besides what we already know?

AND YOUR EARS SHALL HEAR A
WORD BEHIND YOU, SAYING, "THIS
IS THE WAY, WALK IN IT,"

Isaiah 32:21

# #1 - WHEN ENDEAVORING TO BE LED BY THE SPIRIT OF GOD, DON'T THROW OUT YOUR COMMON SENSE!

This one principle alone could save most Christians the majority of mistakes they make. Unfortunately, many of us over-spiritualize our decisions, and as a result ignore plain common sense. I learned this one the hard way early on.

I had just started a new business, and I knew that businesses of my kind (a small sign company) were busier in the summertime than in the wintertime. In spite of that, I chose to hire my first employee my first year of business at the peak of summer activity. It had been a real struggle to get my little business off the ground. After months of prayer, and standing on the promises of God for favor and success, so many jobs finally started coming in that I literally, could not keep up with it. I thought I needed help. So I hired a good friend. (Please note: at no point did I ever hear the Lord tell me to hire an employee. I was just doing what seemed right at the time.)

But fall was just around the corner. No sooner had I hired this individual, than business slacked off. It was grueling for me, and put them in a very uncomfortable situation. I thought I was stepping out on faith. I thought I was being quite spiritual. I thought I had prayed my way, and believed my way, and yes, confessed my way through the hard times. I believed the little burst of activity that finally came was proof I had overcome. I believed things were getting better permanently, which they were. But it did not eliminate natural seasonal highs and lows.

Unfortunately, it was like someone turned off the financial faucet. What little money I had quickly began to dry up. My poor employee got into credit card debt because I couldn't meet payroll. It was embarrassing, stressful, and tested our friendship. But it was a powerful lesson learned—I got experience.

I learned the hard way that just because I was a praying, believing Christian, I was not exempt from normal business highs and lows in my industry. Common sense would have dictated that I just grit my teeth and slug it through the busy season, knowing it would soon slow down. But I overrode common sense, and hired her anyway. (By the way, I did eventually get my friend completely paid off on back wages, and we are still friends, thanks to her graciousness.)

## WINTER CAMP BLUES

A friend of mine had her own special evangelistic ministry which included a summer camp for boys and girls in an Old West setting. They did a lot of horseback riding, and she would hire the best Christian cowboys and cowgirls she could to help run her camp. She needed experienced horsemen to do the job. Because good, experienced cowboys and cowgirls who love the Lord were hard to come by, she felt she needed to keep them hired all year long, even when there were no camps.

Her problem was the same as mine. When winter rolled around, no money was coming in when there are no camps. So basically, keeping on all those employees sitting around with nothing to do, ate up all of her savings and financial reserves. To someone more experienced in business, common sense would have dictated if there's no money coming in, then there's no money for employees. No matter how good they were at their jobs, it would have been better to let them go, and believe God for good employees the following year.

Let's just say things did not turn out well for any of them. Remember when endeavoring to be led by the spirit of God, don't throw out your common sense.

## DON'T QUIT YOUR JOB!

If you feel like God has called you to full-time ministry, don't quit your job until He clearly tells you what the next step is. This should be common sense. I've seen people make this mistake many times. Christians feel a true call to ministry, and they are zealous to launch out and go into action. But they fail to realize that from the call to the fulfilment frequently takes time, sometimes years, before it comes to pass. But they feel they are acting on faith and being obedient to act quickly. It's their way of showing God they love Him and are willing to serve Him.

But common sense says take things one step at a time. Know it's a process and let the Lord lead you. Soon enough it will be clear when it's time to take that leap of faith. Don't leap into the darkness without a little more leading of the Spirit.

## WHAT IS COMMON SENSE?

It may not seem very spiritual to be talking about common sense in the same context of being led by the Spirit. But not using common sense really sets us up to look foolish. By definition common sense is basically good sense and sound judgment in practical matters. It's the ability to use good judgment in making decisions in order to live in a reasonable and safe way. It actually has to be learned, either by experience, or from someone else.

The more knowledge you have about things, the more decisions become a matter of common sense. For example, if you know what poison ivy looks like, and you know the unpleasant effects of topical contact with the plant, it becomes basic common sense not to touch it. But a person without this knowledge cannot make this common sense judgment.

Here are more examples: When you remove a teakettle from the stove, it's common sense to then turn off the burner. Common sense says you shouldn't jump out of an airplane without a parachute. Common sense says if you don't want to go to jail, pay your taxes!

Common sense, however, is not necessarily a collection of universal fixed truths. It can vary state to state, from nation to nation, and culture to culture. What is common sense in North Dakota may not have any relevance in California.

For instance, if you live on a ranch with lots of livestock, it's common sense to make sure all the gates are closed when you leave a pasture so the cattle don't get out. But if you grew up in the city and visited that ranch, it may not even cross your mind how important it is to close the gate.

Most people understand that if you step out in front of a speeding car are likely to get killed. So, common sense dictates that you shouldn't do it. However, a one-year-old doesn't know that a speeding car is deadly. He has to be taught.

Common sense for Christians, interestingly enough, can also be different than it is for unbelievers. This is true for those Christians who know their Bibles well.

## EMOTIONS CAN OVER-RIDE REASON

Some people who are very emotional tend to lack common sense. The reason is the brain produces emotions faster than judgment. Even though difference is just milliseconds, it could be enough for an irrational response to something. Some Christians tend to be very emotional. Mix this with religious zeal, and you have a dangerous combination.

## INTELLIGENCE AND COMMON SENSE

If someone doesn't have regular social interaction, it may be more difficult for them to learn what common sense is and how to use it. This is why very smart people who spend a lot of time by themselves might seem to lack common sense.

Some have said that people with high IQs tend to ignore common sense, which is learned cultural behavior, in favor of reasoning. It might seem smart to them because reasoning is their strength, but can often lead to geniuses coming up with strange responses or behaviors. This is where a Christian who is very intelligent really needs to rely on a knowledge of the Word of God, and not just his intelligence. in decision making. There are several scriptures that warn us about being wise in our own eyes. (1 Corinthians 3:18; Proverbs 3:7)

## COMMON SENSE IN THE BIBLE

The Bible does not actually talk about common sense in the older original versions, such as the King James Version. In newer versions, however, like the message Bible, or the New Living Translation, the word "wisdom" is frequently exchanged with the term "common sense."

So it begs the question: Are wisdom and common sense, the same thing? The Bible has a lot to say about wisdom. We sometimes use a term called "conventional wisdom," which is by definition "commonplace knowledge." Commonplace knowledge seems to be a different way of saying common sense. So we can see why the terms might be interchangeable in the Bible.

Wisdom, however, is more of an age related thing. For instance, you will find many more elders with wisdom, then teenagers. Wisdom is something gained over a period of time. It's what makes a person wise in the soul giving them a clearer understanding about their lives, as well as life in general. This includes past mistakes, failures—their own a others.

For instance, a grandmother may believe a young girl will run into problems if she dates someone who is quite a bit older than her. This is not necessarily common sense, because many people due date older people, and it turns out fine. But if the grandmother had a bad experience herself, or watched some of her girlfriends become emotionally wrecked by older guys, she would have personal wisdom on the subject that deserves consideration. One gains wisdom when the lessons of life influence one in the right direction. And, of course, wisdom also comes from the word of God.

Many times, like in my case, Christians think they are above common sense because, they may believe that they can just use their faith, and override natural consequences others experience. Nothing could be further from the truth. When endeaveroing to follow the leading of the Holy Spirit, considering things that are common sense is one of the first things you can do. If more Christians would just use common sense, they would not get into many of the problems they do.

I've spent a lot of time on this topic. But it's because one of the best pieces of advice I can give you when you are trying to be led by the Spirit of God is don't throw out your common sense!

MY SHEEP HEAR MY VOICE, AND I KNOW THEM, AND THEY FOLLOW ME.

John 10:27

# #2 - BE HONEST WITH YOURSELF AND OTHERS. MAKE SURE YOUR MOTIVES ARE PURE.

Jesus, our example, said "By myself I can do nothing; I judge only as I hear, and my judgment is just, *for I seek not to please myself* but him who sent me." John 5:30 (Emphasis mine.) The King James Version says, "because *I seek not mine own will*, but the will of the Father."

My dad has always hated it when people say to him, "God told me to do…." He would say they were using it as an excuse to get out of doing something they didn't want to do. Because he'd seen it happen so many times, even as a Christian he was completely skeptical of anyone who used that phrase.

If you've been a Christian for very long, you've probably seen it too. It happens in cases like when a person starts a new job that they really love. They will even say God led them to that job, or God told them to take that job. But after a while, things get a little rough. It gets rough enough that they want to quit. They confuse their feelings and emotions with the leading of the Spirit. So they say, "God told me to leave that job."

So which is it? Did he tell you to take the job or not? God is not fickle. He does not change his mind so quickly. If He absolutely, positively told you to take the job, don't you think he knew rough and tough times would come? Just hold on a little while, things will get better.

We must be careful not to use God as an excuse to get out of doing something that suddenly becomes uncomfortable. Be honest with yourself and others. When you claim that you're being led by the spirit of God, make sure, that like Jesus, your motives are pure. Don't seek your own will, but seek the will of the father who has sent you.

I WILL INSTRUCT YOU AND TEACH
YOU IN THE WAY YOU SHOULD GO.

Psalm 32:8

# #3 - DON'T BE LED BY CIRCUMSTANCES.

This is very similar to example in my last point. If we as believers are truly seeking God for direction, and feel we have heard His voice, we must stand firm on the word we heard. We have to understand God has a plan and purpose for His leading, and negative circumstances will have to turn around.

One of the biggest life-altering decisions I ever made was leaving my home state of North Dakota, where I'd lived for many years, and move all the way across the country to North Carolina. It wasn't just a desire, or an emotional decision. I had very clear explicit leading from the Holy Spirit to move.

A good friend of mine gave me a prophetic word that when I got there I was going to face some very rough personal times. It was a bit unnerving when she said, "God's going to get you alone, and jerk the slack out of you. And the only thing that will hold you is that you know that you know that you know God sent you there." She was right on both counts.

One of the leaders in our ministry has shared publicly how she and her husband got a clear word from the Lord about home schooling their four children. Not long after she got started, however, her husband chose another path, and left the family. So Torry was suddenly left with four children under the age of eight to take care of and raise by herself.

When the pastor of her church and the board members found out what it happened, they immediately began to give her advice. They told her she needed to sell her house, put the kids in public school, and go get a job so she could support her family. They told her in no uncertain terms she needed to just forget all her plans because circumstances had changed. In fact, we could say, they were telling her she needed to use "common sense."

My friend said she actually cried when they left. But she wasn't crying for herself. She was crying for them because their God was so small. She knew she had heard from God. She shared, "God knew my husband was going to leave when He told me to home school my children. He hasn't told me anything different just because the circumstances have changed. So I am doing what he told me."

Her oldest son at the time of this writing, is now 15. She has home schooled all of her children from the time he started school. It is one of the happiest families you'll ever meet. The home is full of joy, laughter, creativity, and her children are exceptional students. It is not been easy. She has to believe for financial miracles regularly as she's never gone out and gotten a job. But God has never failed them. She is a prime example of not allowing the circumstances to lead her against the clear word of the Lord for her and her family.

When you know that you know that you know you've heard from God, don't make changes just because the circumstances changed.

CALL TO ME AND I WILL ANSWER
YOU, AND WILL TELL YOU GREAT AND
HIDDEN THINGS THAT YOU HAVE
NOT KNOWN.

Jeremiah 33:3

# #4 - WHEN YOU DON'T KNOW WHAT TO DO, SEEK GODLY COUNSEL.

Sometimes, as heard as we try we simply cannot hear the voice of God on some decisions. We want to hear His voice, but the signal seems to be jammed. There seems to be confusion of which way to go. We need others to help us unjam the signal. God never intended for any of us to live in a vacuum, and none of us know it all. He created us unique, with certain strengths, but also weaknesses. He created us to work in community and in relationships. When it comes to decision making, we each have our blind spots, and it's really a safety feature to seek godly counsel. Don't be so proud that you think you have to figure everything out all by yourself.

Proverbs 15:22 – Plans fail for lack of counsel. With many advisers they succeed.

Proverbs 11:14 – Where there is no counsel, the people fall, but in a multitude of counselors, there is safety.

If you are married, the first person you need to partner

with and listen to the advice of is your spouse. This only works when both parties are truly working together as partners wanting the best for their family. There's no room for selfish motivation, manipulation, pride, and stubbornness. I wish I had a dollar for every testimony I've heard where a Christian husband and wife strongly disagreed on a decision to be made. One of the spouses (usually the husband) would go against the wishes of his wife. They frequently have had to recant, admitting their wife was right.

Of course, this can happen the other way around, but typically the man considers himself the head of the house and will use that as leverage to be the push his decisions through when there is a strong disagreement.

Even if your spouse if not a Christian, don't automatically rule out their opinion, unless it clearly goes against scripture or your Christian convictions. They can still possess good common sense and wisdom about many things. Many times they are more clued into spiritual perspectives than we give them credit for.

## WHAT TO DO IF YOU ARE SINGLE

If you are single, like I am, you need to ask God to surround you with stable, loving, Christian friends (I recommend married couples to be among them) to whom you can safely go for advice when necessary. I have learned over the years, as a woman, God has put uniqueness in the male gender (vice versa if you are a man) which gives them an important alternative perspective on almost everything. I have needed a different perspective, even when things were challenging.

I have often been amazed at the value of the male perspective in my ministry decisions, as well as personal life. I have leaned heavily on my father through the years for this very reason. (Just an aside, but I hope I don't have to say it, but you should **NEVER UNDER ANY CIRCUMSTANCES** meet with someone of the opposite gender without the spouse present.)

But there's a second part to this. If you're going to seek godly counsel, you've got have an open and submissive heart to sincerely listen to what they say, and be ready take their advice even if you don't like what you are hearing. It's okay to get counsel from more than one person, especially if some of the advice makes you uncomfortable. But make sure you are not being self-willed and stubborn by not receiving the counsel you have asked for. I'm not saying you are required to take their advice, but you really need another perspective.

## SEEK WISDOM

Seeking godly counsel is not just about looking just for common sense, but it should be about seeking advice from those who have true godly wisdom. These are people who have experience—sometimes years of experience—in the areas you are struggling in. The obvious: if you're struggling with finances, go to someone who is good with money and budgeting. If you are struggling with decisions about your teenagers, find Christian parents who have successfully raised children who are fully serving God as adults. They know something you could learn from. (Really, this is just more common sense!)

**Please note:** Seeking counsel from others is not the same as taking votes from your friends on which way you should go. I've seen this happen many times. People may want to be led by the spirit of God, but they are not sure if they're hearing clearly. Or more than likely, they don't like what they're hearing. So they go to their friends and take a vote to see what their friends think of the idea. They keep going to more friends until they can find a majority of people who will agree with them. That's not what we're talking about here. Again, you have to check your motives. Don't seek your own will, but the will of the Father.

# #5 - WHEN CONFUSED, GO BACK TO THE LAST PLACE WHERE YOU KNOW FOR SURE YOU HAD CLEAR DIRECTIONS FROM GOD, AND START OVER.

It's easy to make one bad decision after another until things are such a mess, you don't know which way to turn. This even happens when people are sincerely trying to follow the leading of the Lord. It may have begun by overlooking a number of common sense steps in the beginning of the process. Or for lack of experience, they made decisions they did not realize were unwise until the consequences hit.

Sometimes people have come asking me for advice, and their web is so tangled, it's difficult to know what to tell them. It's at times like this, you need to go back to the last place where you know beyond a doubt you heard clearly from God, and you followed it accurately. What happened after that? What decision was made that started you down the wrong path? Like retracing your steps when you lose your car keys, retrace your spiritual steps and see if you can somehow start over in some way at that place. If this is not possible, seek godly counsel, and ask God to show you some common sense steps to help you straighten things out.

# #6 – GET OUT FROM UNDERNEATH THE PRESSURE OF YOUR BAD DECISIONS SO YOU CAN HEAR CLEARLY FROM GOD.

It's nearly impossible to make good choices and decisions when you are buried under pressure of any kind. The worst time to make life altering decisions is when you are under extreme pressure. It's nearly impossible to clearly hear the voice of God when life is caving in around you.

It might not always be possible, but if you can, physically get away from your circumstances even temporarily just to be able to sit in silence, away from the chaos, and pray. Try even if it's just for a few hours at a time. Obviously if you have a family, you can't run away from them. But between the Lord and friends, it will become clear how you can do it in your circumstances.

A young friend of mine one time had found herself in deep financial trouble and nothing seemed to be working out. Every decision seemed to be thrusting her in deeper. The job she was counting on in the big city didn't work out. The scholarship she was hoping to get went to someone else when it seemed to be a certainty. It was her only to way to pay for her college education. Because of lack of experience in business dealings, she was in financial trouble over a house she had invested in, which now had huge repairs needed, and no money to fix them.

Her choices were to stay in the big city she was in at the time and keep trying to find a job when she was already out of money. Or to regroup, move back home for a season with caring parents, get out from underneath as much of the financial pressure as possible, to just seek God for a season.

It takes time to unravel some of the bad decisions we make. But slowly, when we get out from underneath the pressure, we can think more clearly, hear more accurately from the Spirit, and things will began to change.

# #7 – DON'T BE IN A HURRY; NOT TOO FAST / NOT TOO SLOW

I was a radio advertising salesman for a couple of years, and transitioned into running a sign company for thirteen years. I used the same sales skills in both jobs. I learned through daily practice what it took to make a sale. Most of the time, I wanted to close the deal on the first encounter. If the customer wanted to wait and think about, asking me to come back later, or wanted to go home and think about it, my chances of closing that sale dropped dramatically.

When a customer would come in to my sign shop asking for a bid, it looked like the sale was going good. Then for some reason they would begin to back out. I learned to quickly start asking them questions to just keep them talking. I had learned over the years if I could just reengage them in conversation about the project, I could almost find the problem and close the sale.

When I started learning how to be led by the Spirit of God, it actually affected how I approached selling. I was learning how not to be an impulse decision maker, and was building a new habit of looking on "the inside" for the voice of the Spirit for direction before making decisions. Especially when my customer was another Christian, I found myself being very conscious of not trying to talk them into a sale unless I knew they were ready to buy.

By nature, I was a very spontaneous person, and made a lot of decisions impulsively. When I took seriously learning to be led by the Spirit, I had to be very careful not to fall into old habits. I learned in making important decisions, especially —like buying a house or a vehicle—to build an image on the inside of spirit over a period of time, so when I went shopping I wouldn't get talked into something I would regret later.

There's a flip side to this issue. And it involves the personality types which take so much time to make a decision; they actually never get around to deciding at all. They simply put it on the back burner until they miss real opportunities and genuine leadings of the Spirit. Since this is not my inherent problem, I can't speak into it in the same way I can on impulsiveness. But individuals in this category need to learn it is definitely possible to wait too long, and miss what God has for them. I know many people who have done this.

I don't know if they are individuals who just can't make up their minds, or they live in fear of making a mistake. But this is as problematic as making spontaneous decisions. In thinking of individuals in this category, many of them would have done well to listen to their spouses who God gave them to balance them out. Many of them overlooked some good spiritual common sense or natural common sense, and would not seek godly counsel from others.

# #8 - BUILD AN IMAGE IN YOUR HEART

I could write a whole book just on this point alone. It has been such a proven winner for me. It has retrained me from much of my impulsiveness, and helped me make decisions which have turned out to be excellent choices for years. In learning to build an image of what I wanted or needed, it made it easier not to violate that image when decision time came. This would also help those who have a hard time making decisions. If they had a carefully built image in their hearts, it would be easier for them to recognize the hand of God when they see it. Again, it may not seem very spiritual in and of itself. But go back to what God asked Jeremiah when He asked, "What do you see?"

One of the principles I learned, even when trying to be led by the Spirit of God, is He allows us to choose many things ourselves in making decisions. Our imaginations are God given, and even something that seems like day-dreaming, can be a spiritual experience if you're heart is fixed on doing the will of God. Visualizing things is not a New Age principle. They are counterfeiting what God designed for us as His people to use.

If you listen closely to the principles I use in this story, you will see it encompasses common sense, wisdom, putting myself in a position where circumstance don't rule the situation, avoiding spontaneous, fast decisions, and following peace.

It had to do with the first house I bought. I had been renting the upstairs of a duplex house for five years. I actually ran my new sign company from it, with my landlord's blessing.

But eventually I wanted to buy my own house. I began to realize what a great idea it was to have duplex for someone like me. Among other things, I loved the idea of having a renter who could help me pay my mortgage while I was till getting my business established.

I began dreaming and visualizing all of the things I would like in a house based on my experience of living in one. It had to be an over under duplex, with separate entrances, separate furnaces, three bedrooms up, and three bedrooms down (very rare in my area at the time.) But I knew having all those things would make it so much easier to find renters. It also needed to have washer and dryer hookups both upstairs and down.

I wanted a double garage so both my renter and I could have a garage space. This was also a selling feature for a rental, I believed. I built this image over a two or three year period of time. It was a solid image—I had anon-negotiable list and a negotiable list. As I added an item to my list, I learned to check in my spirit, and see if it brought peace or turmoil in my heart.

Then there was my personal wish list which would make a house an even sweeter deal. I wanted a nice big yard, mature trees, near the city center, a paved driveway. Having a beautiful brick exterior would be the icing on the cake, even though I didn't think I had enough money for a home like that.

The day came when I finally had my down payment. It

dictated what price I could pay for a house, and therefore what the monthly payments could be.

This is where a non-negotiable came in. The monthly payments could not exceed $650. When I looked down inside my spirit and thought about making monthly payments, I had a great peace about this amount. If I toyed with $675 or $700 or higher, which meant I could buy a nicer house, I got an uncomfortable red light, or that tight, uneasy feeling in my stomach. I would go back and think about $650, and my peace level returned. I realized this was the voice of the Spirit of God guiding me in this very important part of the buying process.

When I thought about my list of non-negotiables, negotiables, and the price, I felt a deep peace. It was calmness, and an assurance all this was OK with God. (Remember, the voice of God is not always a voice—many times it's a feeling on the inside.)

So, armed with this information, I called up a realtor friend of mine, told her exactly what I wanted, and how much I could spend. The very first house she took me to met all of my duplex requirements on my list to a tee. My eyes popped! Not only did it have the duplex requirements, but it had everything on my wish list too. It was an adorable little house fully bricked from top to bottom, huge yard, double garage, with a paved driveway, and lots of mature trees. It was also at the exact price I could afford, including the size of the monthly payments. It was as though they custom built that house just for me!

Because I had carefully built the exact image of what I wanted in a house, I didn't have to fast and pray to ask God if this was the one. I had already done that work. As we pulled into the driveway, in my spirit I knew this was my house! I just knew it. I didn't have to pray about putting in an offer.

But there was just one little glitch. Because I was new

in business, I did not have a long enough credit history to get a loan from the bank. So I needed the seller to give me a contract for deed, having them finance me and carry the loan. They were a retired couple, and they owed no money on it, so they could easily do this.

But they didn't want to. My realtor tried to talk them into it, but they wouldn't budge. We left, and surprisingly I wasn't upset. I had peace. This was my house no matter what the circumstances looked like. I just lifted it up to God, and said, God you know that's my house. But we can't force them to give me the contract. So I don't know how you're going to do it, but I'm leaving it your hands.

A few days later I ran into a friend who flipped houses for a living. He and I had talked real estate many times. I told him about this house and how it had everything I wanted.

"Was it at 511 S. Anderson Street?" he asked.

Shocked, I said, "Yes! How did you know?"

He replied, "Because my partner and I looked it, but couldn't make the right deal with the sellers, so we left. But I remember thinking; this house would be perfect for Becky!"

It blew me away. "The only problem is," I told him, "they won't give me a contract for deed on."

"Really?" He said. "They were willing to go contract for deed with us."

Armed with that interesting new information, I quickly told my realtor, who immediately went back to the sellers. She revealed she had found out they were willing to carry the note before, so wouldn't they please consider doing it again? Miraculously she was able to make the deal. I got my perfect house at the perfect price. It matched perfectly the image I carried in my spirit. I owned that house for 19 years. It proved to be a blessing to me over and over again. Eventually, I stopped renting the basement and started Kids in Ministry International. I operated KIMI out of the basement apartment for about 5 years. God knew what I needed and He taught me to build an image in my heart.

It was like he had asked me, "Becky, what do you see?"

"This is what I see this Lord!" And I described my house to Him.

"You have spoken well," He said. "And I'm watching over my word to perform it."

WHOEVER IS OF GOD HEARS THE
WORDS OF GOD.

John 8:47

# #9 – MAKE A LIST

There's something about just writing something down on paper that helps clear things up. When things are clear, it's much easier to make wise decisions, and be more confident one is being led by the Spirit. Here's a simple, but good example which happened to me.

We have had family conferences at the Fire Center (our ministry facility) since we moved into it in 2007. They were often the highlight of our ministry year. Families would come from all over the USA, and even from other countries, to participate. Our crowds were good, and the presence of the Holy Spirit was powerful.

When the recession hit, we got hit too. Within two years our income dropped dramatically. Our faithful families were also affected, and almost overnight attendance at our conferences dropped off. At the time of this writing, we are still in recession, and things have stayed economically about the same.

I debated for three or four years whether we should keep having the family conferences, when the attendance had been so low. But I kept hanging on thinking, well, we have this beautiful building, we need to be doing something with it. I would reason this is where our international headquarters for the ministry is. How can I go and hold conferences in a lot of other states and countries, but not do anything here at home? And finally, how can we let down the handful of families who live here in ND and come faithfully every year?

I went round and round in my head about it. I discussed it with my staff many times, but never come to solid conclusion. One day, I felt impressed by the Spirit to take a piece of paper, draw a line down the middle and write down all the reasons we should continue holding the conferences on one side, and all the reasons we shouldn't on the other. This is a principle many people use, whether they are Christians or not. So I'm not introducing anything new. But we can safely put it in our arsenal of excellent ideas to help us make good, sound decisions when trying to hear the voice of God clearly.

It didn't take long for me to arrive at a conclusion, because did you notice what was nowhere on my list? I had never actually heard God say we should continue. I had a list of reasons in the natural which seemed reasonable, but I did not have the word of the Lord it this was His will. We can sometimes wear ourselves out doing things He never told us to do. They aren't wrong, but they take up time and energy unnecessarily. Just because something was the will of God in the past, doesn't mean we keep doing it forever.

In this case when I simply prayed about, I couldn't seem to hear His voice clearly on the issue. It was when I wrote it down on paper, things cleared up and became obvious.

So we immediately cancelled the meetings. We will gladly resume at any time we get a clear word from God on it.

# #10 - DON'T BE LED BY PROPHETIC WORDS

This is a tough one. I believe in prophetic words. I give prophetic words to people. I have a folder full of prophetic words I've kept over the years that's an inch thick. I highly value those words, and go back and look at them from time to time to remind myself of God's personal words to me. But I don't make my decisions based on prophetic words.

This is an entire subject all of its own, and so many excellent Bible teachers have written and spoken on this topic that I don't want to spend a lot of time on it here. But let me say in my experience, prophetic words and dreams have come as confirmation to what I was already carrying in my heart.

I honestly can't think of any time where I based a decision solely on a prophetic word. Many times they alerted me to things I had not thought of before. They cleared out a lot of cobwebs and brought spiritual clarity to me at times, revealed the significance of things I my past. They reminded me of God's love and care for me.

Sometimes they had warnings in them that alerted me to situation's coming ahead. Some were quite dramatic. I didn't always know what to do with them until they actually unfolded. But being forewarned was quite helpful. But I've never made a decision based solely on a prophetic word.

I have always believed words from the Lord were invitations. He was telling me what He saw for my future, what He wanted me to walk in, the plans He had for me, but many times they were conditional "If you will do this, I will do that in your life." Many times it was a heart I needed. If I would have gone out and tried to make those things happen, I would have fallen flat on my face. Many times prophetic words are for years down the road.

God definitely speaks to us through dreams and prophetic words. But we need to be careful we have the right interpretation and not make assumptions that really cater to our egos and flesh causing us to get out ahead of God, or make wrong choices. Even if you are absolutely convinced a prophetic word is giving you direction, seek counsel. Accept wise advice from those who have experience in the prophetic, and see what they think. Especially if it is a life-altering decision.

# #11 – GO WITH YOUR FIRST IMPRESSION

Think back to the Garden of Eden when God walked and talked with Adam and Eve. He told them very clearly they were not to eat from the Tree of the Knowledge of Good and Evil. But later another voice came. It told them just the opposite. This voice muddied the water, and gave a confusing signal. If Adam and Eve would have listened to the first voice, they could have avoided a lot of heartache.

I have found over the years when I am praying about something or making decisions, the first thought that comes to my mind is usually the Lord. When additional thoughts come, I start getting confused. Which one is right? Is this other one from God? Is this my own thoughts? Is the Devil trying to confuse me? Which one is God? If I will go back to the first thought that came to me, it usually turns out to be the right one.

Believe it or not, I actually practice this one when I'm playing dominos with my parents. When it's my turn and I have to draw a domino, I look at the pile and see which piece is my first impression to pick. When it doesn't come to me quickly, I will try to practice the principle of being "drawn" like a magnet to the right piece.

In Hebrews 5:24 Paul indicates that by practice or constant use we can train ourselves to distinguish between good and evil. In other words we can exercise our spirits to be discerning. I believe this includes practicing being led by the Spirit.

It's an interesting exercise. I don't necessarily use it to help me win, but simply to practice to see if I pick the right domino at the time I need it.

You can use the idea of making a list with this tip as well. When you have more than one thought coming to you, once again, make a list. Only this time, number them. Which idea was the first one that came to you? Put a number one beside it. Do the same with all the other conflicting thoughts.

Then read each one individually. Stop, close your eyes and think about it. In a place of quietness, look down in your heart. What do you feel when you think about idea #1? #2? #3? Is it a warm, peaceful feeling? Or do you sense even the slightest bit of uneasiness. Write down what you feel beside each one of the thoughts. Then go back and do this again over your first idea. What do you sense?

Most of the time, you will find your first impression is the one you should go with.

# #12 - PAY ATTENTION TO IMPRESSIONS THAT KEEP COMING BACK TO YOU

Again, I could relate many personal examples, because this happens a lot to me. But I'll give you just a short example. When I am getting ready for a ministry trip, and I am packing my suitcase full of object lessons, I always have my series of lessons already made up. The visuals I need are written right into the messages, so when I go to my prop room, all I have to do is gather them up and throw them in.

But many times as I'm packing, I'll get an impression I am supposed to take an object with me that I am not planning to teach on. It's such a soft subtle nudge, that's it's extremely easy to shrug off. A few minutes later, I get an image of the object in my mind again. I'll mentally argue, "But I'm not teaching on the subject, I don't need it."

Sometimes the impression will come back to me four or five times throughout my packing day. You'd think I'd learn! But many times I have shrugged past it. And you guessed it. When I get to my meetings, suddenly I will have an inspiration to throw in the teaching on that subject which I don't normally include, and I need those particular object lessons.

So then I either have to go without, or scramble to get to a store at the last minute and try to find what I need. I have come to realize the still small, gentle voice of the Spirit, comes in a recurring visual in my thoughts. "Here—you need to pack this."

I'm getting better, but I still blow it from time to time. It's learning not to override His quiet, small, never pushy, but sometimes persistent voice. Pay attention when it happens to you.

# # 13 – DON'T GO PAST YOUR PEACE

I've actually alluded to this in combination with several of the other tips on being led by the spirit. But it really is a subject all its own. When making decisions learn to be continually looking down into your heart—or your spirit—checking to see what you are feeling on the inside. Is there any unrest or turmoil you notice? Is there a knot in your stomach? A yucky feeling? An uneasiness of any kind? Or is there a calmness and peace when you think about doing a particular thing? This is something you can actually practice on a daily basis.

God leads us by peace. When you have lost your peace in a situation, you need to back up to the point where you still were feel peace in your heart.

This is a cardinal rule—when being led by the Spirit of God, DON'T GO PAST YOUR PEACE. Whatever the situation is, stop and work the issue out. Sometimes it was a misunderstanding, or something you heard wrong. If it involves another person, talk it out. Many times, your peace level will return after new information is given to clarify something. But the rule of thumb is, don't go past your peace.

# IN CONCLUSION

While there may be others, these are key principles which will help you discern the voice of God and make better decisions. Here is the list we discussed in this book.

#1 -  When endeavoring to be led by the spirit of God, don't throw out your common sense!
#2 -  The honest with yourself and others. Make sure your motives are pure.
#3 -  Don't be led by circumstances.
#4 -  When you don't know what to do seek godly counsel.
#5 -  When you feel confused, go back to where you last got clear directions from God, and start over from there.
#6 -  Get out from underneath the pressure of your bad decisions so you can hear clearly from God.
#7 -  Don't be in a hurry – Not too fast / Not too slow
#8 -  Build an image in your heart
#9 -  Make a list
#10 - Don't be led by prophetic words
#11 - Go with your first impression
#12 - Pay attention to impressions that keep coming back to your mind
#13 - Don't go past your peace

Made in the USA
Charleston, SC
04 January 2016